Elevate Your Assertiveness
The Art of Commanding Respect

Felicity Jill Mcdonald

Table of Contents

1. Introduction 2
2. Understanding Assertiveness: More Than Just Confidence 3
   - 2.1. Defining Assertiveness 3
   - 2.2. Assertiveness Versus Aggressiveness and Passivity 4
   - 2.3. Assertiveness: A Radical Shift in Perspective 4
   - 2.4. The Empowered Self: The Heartbeat of Assertiveness 5
   - 2.5. Building Block of Assertiveness: Self-Esteem 5
   - 2.6. The Journey Beyond: Assertiveness and Transformation ... 6
3. Decoding the Psychology of Respect 8
   - 3.1. The Nature of Respect 8
   - 3.2. A Cloth of Many Colours: Types of Respect 8
   - 3.3. The Precursor: Self-Respect 9
   - 3.4. Respect as an Assertiveness Tool 9
   - 3.5. The Path to Earning Respect 10
   - 3.6. The Butterfly Effect: Spreading Respect 10
4. Busting Myths: Common Misconceptions About Assertiveness 12
   - 4.1. Disentangling Assertiveness and Aggression 12
   - 4.2. Clarifying The Link Between Assertiveness and Self-esteem .. 13
   - 4.3. Overcoming The Illusion of Confrontation 13
   - 4.4. Assertiveness and the Unreality of Universal Acceptance .. 14
5. Assertiveness and Emotional Intelligence: The Unseen Link 15
   - 5.1. The Foundation Stones of Emotional Intelligence 15
   - 5.2. Building Assertiveness Through Emotional Intelligence .. 16
   - 5.3. Emotional Intelligence as the Bedrock of Assertive Communication ... 17
   - 5.4. Conclusion 17
6. Fine-tuning Your Verbal Communication Skills 19
   - 6.1. The Essence of Verbal Communication 19

- 6.2. Honing Articulation Skills 20
- 6.3. Emphasizing Tone and Inflection 20
- 6.4. Mastering Language Accuracy 21
- 6.5. Contextual Considerations 21
- 6.6. Displaying Assertiveness in Disagreeable Situations 21
- 7. Non-Verbal Communication: The Silent Conductor of Respect . . . 23
  - 7.1. Unraveling Non-Verbal Communication 23
  - 7.2. The Semiotics of Body Language 24
  - 7.3. The Power of Facial Expressions 24
  - 7.4. The Impact of Eye Contact 24
  - 7.5. Navigating Personal Space and Proximity 25
  - 7.6. Deciphering Gestures and Touch 25
  - 7.7. The Resonance of Paralanguage 25
  - 7.8. Bringing It All Together: Non-Verbal Assertiveness 26
- 8. Assertiveness in Conflict Resolution: Winning Without Fighting . 27
  - 8.1. Assertiveness: A Non-combative Approach 27
  - 8.2. The Psychology of Assertive Conflict Resolution 28
  - 8.3. The Techniques of Assertive Conflict Resolution 28
  - 8.4. Conflict Resolution Styles: Comparison with Assertiveness . . 29
  - 8.5. Practical Tips on Incorporating Assertiveness in Conflict Management 29
- 9. Cultivating Respect in Professional Spaces 31
  - 9.1. Setting Expectations and Boundaries 31
  - 9.2. Assertive Communication: The Professional Power Tool . . . 31
  - 9.3. The Power of Active Listening 32
  - 9.4. Displaying Empathy in Conflict Resolution 32
  - 9.5. Building a Leadership Persona 32
  - 9.6. Assertiveness and Team Dynamics 33
  - 9.7. Assertive Email Communication 33
- 10. Elevating Personal Relationships With Assertiveness 34

10.1. Understanding Assertiveness in Personal Relationships 34
10.2. The Power of "I" Statements in Assertiveness 35
10.3. Implementing Assertiveness in Relationship Conflicts 35
10.4. The Impact of Non-Verbal Assertiveness in Personal Relationships 36
10.5. Sustaining Assertive Communication in Personal Relationships 36
11. Sustaining Your Assertive Journey: Maintaining Momentum and Progress 38
11.1. Reflective Practice: Evaluating Your Experiences 38
11.2. Maintenance Strategies: Keeping the Momentum Alive 39
11.3. Tracking Your Progress: Navigating the Assertiveness Map . 40

Speak clearly, if you speak at all; carve every word before you let it fall.

— Oliver Wendell Holmes Sr.

Chapter 1. Introduction

Welcome, esteemed reader, to a unique exploration of personal transformation! In our special report, "Elevate Your Assertiveness: The Art of Commanding Respect," we unravel the fabric behind commanding presence and fearless speaking, offering a look deep into the heart of assertiveness. This empowering resource is far from your average self-help guide - it is a potent blend of scientifically-backed research and practical exercises to help you forge respect in every interaction, both professional and personal. Regardless of your current confidence levels, our report illuminates pathways to amplify your voice, helping you stand tall amidst the crowd. Whether you're a blooming introvert or a seasoned conversation veteran, let this be your golden ticket - a captivating journey into transforming your communication style. Buckle up and prepare to unlock the power of assertiveness, drawing respect like a magnet! This report isn't merely a read; it's an experience that promises to fill you with enthusiasm and optimism about your future interactions. Why wait? Let's dive in and ascend together on this voyage of discovery—elevating assertiveness, commanding respect, and changing lives!

Chapter 2. Understanding Assertiveness: More Than Just Confidence

Assertiveness is more than a simple display of confidence; it involves a complex interplay of inner belief, outward expression, and mutual interaction - all coming together to create powerful and impactful communication. This is a factor that helps an individual stand tall amidst a crowd, relentlessly voicing out their thoughts and ideas without stepping over the rights of others. You might wonder how assertiveness differs from being dominant or assertive, and therein lies the journey we aim to embark upon in this chapter.

2.1. Defining Assertiveness

In the simplest way, assertiveness can be defined as a communication skill that allows an individual to express their feelings, thoughts, beliefs, and standpoints in an open manner, while also being fully considerate of the perspectives and feelings of others. This straightforward definition, however, belies the complexity and impact of this skill.

Becoming assertive is about creating a balance in your interactions. Picture a string instrument, perfectly tuned – it doesn't waver aimlessly; nor does it overwhelm with an overly loud sound. Similarly, an assertive individual neither falls silent in the face of adversity nor bulldozes through others' opinions. This balance allows assertiveness to promote positivity and understanding in interactions, fostering healthy relationships and drawing respect from every quarter.

2.2. Assertiveness Versus Aggressiveness and Passivity

To fully appreciate the nature of assertiveness, it is vital to distinguish it from aggressiveness and passivity—the extreme ends of the communication spectrum. People often misconstrue assertiveness as being aggressive or overbearing. However, these two styles couldn't be further apart.

Aggressiveness, unlike assertiveness, involves expressing one's thoughts and desires without valuing or considering the rights, thoughts, or feelings of others. It is a win-lose approach where the individual seeks to dominate the conversation, often leading to contention and negative reactions.

On the other end of the spectrum is passivity. Passive individuals often avoid expressing their own feelings or defending their rights, allowing others to overshadow their viewpoints. While this might help avoid immediate conflict, it often leads to long-term resentment and a lack of self-respect.

Assertiveness strikes a balance between these extremes. It is a win-win communication style where an individual respects their own rights and expresses them effectively while also respecting and considering the rights and feelings of others.

2.3. Assertiveness: A Radical Shift in Perspective

Understanding and embracing assertiveness requires a radical shift in perspective. Assertiveness is born out of mutual respect, empathy, and emotional integrity. This shift extends beyond ourselves to understanding and acknowledging the rights and boundaries of others. Mastering assertiveness does not equate to winning every conversation, but seeks to transform conversations into bridges for understanding and progress.

Grasping assertiveness thus involves expanding our definitions of success, acceptance, and influence. It's an acceptance of our personal abilities and limitations and the courage to express them without fear of judgment or rejection. Successful communication isn't a measure of how often or loud one can speak, but the quality of connections and understanding one fosters through meaningful interactions.

2.4. The Empowered Self: The Heartbeat of Assertiveness

Beneath its external application lies the empowering and transformative self-journey of assertiveness. Assertiveness is not a facade one can put on; it's a reflection of strong self-belief, understanding, and acceptance. It's about creating a persona that upholds one's values, respects others, and communicates with openness and empathy.

This journey inward is what differentiates assertiveness from a mere display of confidence. Confidence speaks to how we feel about our abilities; assertiveness, on the contrary, translates this inner belief into outward expression, striking a balance between self-assurance and respect for others.

2.5. Building Block of Assertiveness: Self-Esteem

While dissecting the nature of assertiveness, it's impossible to overlook the pivotal role of self-esteem. Assertiveness, at its core, is the result of firm self-esteem and respect—forged from the acceptance of personal worth, pride in one's abilities, and a healthy respect for personal boundaries.

People with high self-esteem find it easier to assert themselves because they understand their value and aren't afraid to represent it. Self-esteem allows individuals to set and respect personal boundaries, express their needs assertively, and reject unfavorable or disrespectful treatment from others.

In sculpting an assertive personality, one needs to nurture their self-esteem first. This robust demeanor will reflect the inner commitment to personal values and create a powerful, yet empathetic, assertive voice.

2.6. The Journey Beyond: Assertiveness and Transformation

Assertiveness is not a quick-fix or a one-time event. It is a transformative journey that alters personal paradigms and interpersonal relationships. It is a life skill that, when mastered, can bring about dramatic changes in personal and professional life.

This transformation begins with self-awareness and self-respect, followed by improved communication and conflict-resolution skills. The journey of assertiveness ultimately leads to the creation of mutually respectful relationships, boosting overall life satisfaction and personal growth.

In the end, assertiveness isn't about just dawning a cloak of confidence; it's about tipping the scales of interaction in favor of mutual respect, empathy, and understanding. It forms a solid foundation on which to build stronger relationships—where each interaction becomes an avenue for growth and mutual respect—a crucial first step towards commanding respect.

As we advance through the other chapters of this text, we'll delve deeper into practical steps, techniques, and exercises to cultivate and polish your assertiveness skills, enriching your interactions, and ultimately, raising the bar for your personal and professional communication.

Chapter 3. Decoding the Psychology of Respect

Respect often exists as an abstract construct in our minds, yet it profoundly shapes how we engage with the world and how the world engages with us. Unraveling its intricate anatomy entails going beyond the surface level of common definitions and interpretations, plunging right into the matrix of the psychology behind respect.

3.1. The Nature of Respect

Respect, in its most quintessential form, refers to the feeling of deep admiration we hold for someone, stemming from their possessed qualities such as abilities, achievements, or inherent values. It is an acknowledgement of the other person's worth and significance. Simply put, respect is the language of human dignity.

However, the concept of respect doesn't merely rest within the borders of views and attitudes. Its impact seeps into interlinked fields including, but not limited to, our decision-making process, conflict resolution strategies, and relationship management skills. It fosters mutual understanding, nurtures compassion, and cultivates an environment of positive engagement.

3.2. A Cloth of Many Colours: Types of Respect

Respect knits together numerous facets, each contributing to the overall understanding of this complex psychological construct. The main types of respect are:

- **Inherent Respect:** This level of respect is accorded to every individual by virtue of their humanity. It encapsulates the belief

in the inviolable dignity and worth of all human beings.
- **Earned Respect:** This form of respect is not given, but achieved. It is the admiration and esteem one garners through personal accomplishments, ethical conduct, or demonstrated competence.
- **Self-respect:** This variety of respect is intrinsic and refers to the valuation of one's own worth, honour, and dignity.

3.3. The Precursor: Self-Respect

Self-respect acts as the foundational bedrock upon which all forms of respect are built. It is a reflection of one's understanding and acceptance of one's intrinsic value. Self-respect propels individuals to seek environments that honour their worth and to communicate assertively. Furthermore, it bolsters resilience, steering us towards a healthy and productive lifestyle aligned with our self-set boundaries.

When self-respect is present, individuals naturally project the vibe of being valuable and deserving of respect from others. It imbues interactions with dignity, encouraging others to meet us at our level of self-commitment and respect.

3.4. Respect as an Assertiveness Tool

Respect and assertiveness are deeply intertwined. Assertiveness rests upon the foundation of respect—self-respect and respect towards others. Conversely, employing assertive communication can foster respect. By clearly expressing thoughts, feelings, and needs without violating the rights of others, we engage in a dialogue that commands respect. By demonstrating that we respect our own boundaries, we simultaneously model the treatment that we expect from others.

Respect is an instrumental asset in establishing assertiveness. By comprehending its psychological underpinnings, we can harness its potential benefits, leading to enhanced assertiveness, better communication, and improved relationships.

3.5. The Path to Earning Respect

Crafting an identity and aura that commands respect aligns directly with the practices of being assertive. It's essential to remember that genuine respect cannot be demanded — it must be earned. Here are some ways to cultivate earned respect:

- **Knowledge and Competence:** Honing skills and continually amassing knowledge in a chosen sphere promotes admiration and respect. Steadfast dedication to learning and striving for expertise undeniably captivates people's respect.
- **Honesty and Integrity:** Being truthful and committed to moral and ethical principles fosters deep respect. Authenticity generates trust, a vital component of respect.
- **Reliability:** Consistency and reliability instill faith and draw respect. When individuals consistently deliver on their promises and stay true to their words, they accumulate respect as a byproduct.
- **Empathy:** Displaying a genuine understanding of others' feelings and perspectives commands respect. It conveys the message that you value and respect their emotions and experiences.

3.6. The Butterfly Effect: Spreading Respect

Once we've decoded the psychology of respect and learned how to command it, the journey doesn't end there. Instead, it evolves into a ripple-effect, or a spread to magnitude. By engaging others with admiration and treating them with worth, we become messengers of respect, leading by example.

In conclusion, understanding and implementing respect is a vital stepping stone in the journey of becoming more assertive. By fostering self-respect, honing qualities deserving of earned respect, and treating others with inherent respect, we construct a solid foundation for assertiveness. Learning to use respect as an assertiveness tool not only enhances our communication but brings fulfillment to our relationships, personal development, and professional growth.

Chapter 4. Busting Myths: Common Misconceptions About Assertiveness

In the realm of effective communication and self-expression, assertiveness occupies a central place. However, it is critical to acknowledge that surrounding assertiveness, there swirls a thick cloud of myths and mistaken beliefs, which we endeavor to dispel in this chapter.

4.1. Disentangling Assertiveness and Aggression

Perhaps the most common misconception about assertiveness is its incorrect association with aggression. Many people conflate the two, but this couldn't be further from the truth. Assertiveness and aggression are not two sides of the same coin; rather, they represent two fundamentally different approaches to communication. The distinction is crucial, as swapping one for the other can derail the pathway to communication success.

Aggression is marked by dominating conversations, trampling on the rights of others, and resorting to manipulation or intimidation, to make one's point. It triggers hostility and fear, creating a negative, potentially adversarial environment. In contrast, assertiveness aims for open, honest, and balanced communication, respecting not just one's own rights, but also those of others. It generates an atmosphere of mutual respect and understanding, leading to constructive interactions.

The core principle of assertiveness is the equitable sharing of communication space, an acknowledgment of everyone's fundamental right to express themselves. An assertive communicator ensures their viewpoint is heard, without infringing on the conversational rights of others.

4.2. Clarifying The Link Between Assertiveness and Self-esteem

Another widespread myth is that assertiveness is exclusively the realm of the self-assured, a fallacy suggesting that those with low self-esteem can never be assertive. This notion is incorrect and disempowering. Assertiveness and self-esteem, while intertwined, are not mutually exclusive states. Anyone, regardless of their current level of self-esteem, can learn and integrate assertiveness into their communication style.

Assertiveness does not originate solely from self-esteem; it also has roots in self-awareness, empathy, understanding, and patience. Developing assertiveness can, in fact, be a prelude to fostering a healthier self-esteem. As individuals gain proficiency in assertive communication, they inevitably grow in self-confidence, leading to a boost in self-esteem.

4.3. Overcoming The Illusion of Confrontation

Assertiveness is often misconstrued as an invitation for conflict or a predisposition toward confrontation. This illusion shields the true face of assertiveness: a communication skill promoting harmony, understanding, and respect. Viewers through the lens of confrontation fail to perceive its essence — achieving a win-win situation.

Assertive individuals do not invite conflict; instead, they strive for open, honest and respectful communication. They address issues head-on but do so in a manner that respects other people's viewpoints. Avoidance of conflict can often lead to miscommunication and grudges, affecting the quality of relationships and interactions. By actively voicing thoughts and opinions without causing discomfort or harm, assertiveness minimizes misunderstanding and fosters harmonious relationships.

4.4. Assertiveness and the Unreality of Universal Acceptance

A final, and particularly potent, misconception about assertiveness is the assumption that it will lead to universal acceptance. This misconception paints assertiveness as a tool to get everyone to agree with everything one says. However, this is an unrealistic expectation.

The purpose of assertiveness is not to force consensus but to create a platform for understanding and mutual respect. It is important to recognize that people will always possess diverse opinions. Assertiveness promotes the acknowledgment and acceptance of differences while ensuring that individual voices, including one's own, are heard and respected.

In conclusion, assertiveness, far from being a conduit of aggression, a show of conceit, a spark for confrontation, or a tool for universal agreement, represents a path to open, balanced interaction. It is a communication skill that respects everyone's rights to express their feelings and opinions, leading to a mutual understanding. Representing assertiveness correctly is fundamental to leveraging its potential in enhancing our professional and personal relationships. By debunking these misconceptions, we see the tool of assertiveness for what it truly is: a guide to navigating the avenue of communication, creating harmony, and cultivating respect.

Chapter 5. Assertiveness and Emotional Intelligence: The Unseen Link

Let's begin with a fundamental truth: Assertiveness and emotional intelligence coexist in an intricate dance, each moving and shifting in response to the other, inextricably intertwined, though the link between them might be unseen to the layman eye. As we progress, you'll uncover the profound ways in which your journey toward assertiveness is intertwined with emotional intelligence and how these twin powers can complement and balance each other.

5.1. The Foundation Stones of Emotional Intelligence

Emotional intelligence (EQ), a term popularized by psychologist Daniel Goleman, encapsulates five core elements: self-awareness, self-regulation, motivation, empathy, and social skills. Let's delve into each facet to comprehend their relevance to the larger picture of assertiveness.

1. **Self-awareness:** This is an understanding of one's emotions, strengths, weaknesses, drives, values, and goals. When one is self-aware, they understand how their emotions affect their actions, and this is the first step towards assertiveness. With heightened self-awareness, you can identify your emotional responses, discern why you might be feeling a certain way, and how it influences your interactions.

2. **Self-regulation:** The capacity to control or redirect one's disruptive impulses and moods bears witness to the realm of self-regulation. In the context of assertiveness, it equips you to

express your needs and desires without letting emotions cloud your communication, hence, ensuring respectful exchange.

3. **Motivation:** The drive to achieve for the sake of achievement is motivation. It is the fuel that propels assertiveness, compelling you to voice your thoughts and opinions despite discomfort or fear.

4. **Empathy:** The ability to understand others' emotional makeup and treating them accordingly is empathy. It complements assertiveness by helping you convey your needs and thoughts while considering and respecting others' feelings.

5. **Social skills:** This refers to proficiency in managing relationships and building networks. As a critical element of assertiveness, it empowers you to foster connections based on mutual respect.

5.2. Building Assertiveness Through Emotional Intelligence

Studying these underpinnings of emotional intelligence gifts us with a roadmap to build assertiveness. Let's delve into practical steps you can undertake to harness these elements in your assertiveness journey.

. **Cultivate Mindfulness:** Mindfulness, an exercise of sitting in silence, focusing on your breath, thoughts, and emotions is a powerful technique to bolster self-awareness. By observing without judgment, you gain insight into your emotional contours, preparing the ground for assertive behavior.

. **Practice Emotional Regulation:** Emotional regulation can be honed by creating a mental buffer before reacting to emotional trigger points. This can involve techniques like counting to ten, deep breathing, or even stepping away from the situation momentarily.

. **Ignite Your Intrinsic Motivation:** Intrinsic motivation is the most potent kind of motivation since it originates from within. Identify what drives you, what are your passions, and use those strong emotional connections to fuel your assertiveness.

. **Exercise Empathy:** Empathic communication is pivotal for assertiveness. Freely express your viewpoint while considering others' feelings. This requires active listening and resonating with the emotions of your conversational partner.

. **Develop Social Skills:** Engage in social activities to hone your social skills. Small actions like maintaining eye contact, attentive listening, and effective verbal communication contribute to growing assertiveness.

5.3. Emotional Intelligence as the Bedrock of Assertive Communication

Harnessing emotional intelligence is not just about being assertive; it's the difference that allows assertiveness to rest on a foundation of respect for others' boundaries, emotions, and perspectives. An individual with high emotional intelligence will not only voice their needs but will do so while profusely respecting others' feelings. They would phrase their opinions in such a way that the communication would seem less of a demand and more of an assertive request. This balance of conveying your thoughts without running roughshod over others' feelings is the secret to commanding respect.

5.4. Conclusion

Journeying through the rich landscape of emotional intelligence and unveil its inherent link to assertiveness brings a profound learning experience. Building emotional intelligence equips one with the tools needed to be assertively diplomatic and respectful, turning every interaction into a harmonious dance of words. Therefore, integrating emotional intelligence and assertiveness can become a powerful mechanism for healthy, respectful interpersonal communication. As we conclude, we're left with an insight that illuminates the core truth of this intriguing exploration—the unseen link between assertiveness and emotional intelligence is more like a lustrous pearl waiting to be discovered within each of us. It is a journey worth embarking on—a journey of awareness, understanding, and ultimately, a journey of transformative growth. May you walk with the wisdom of emotional intelligence lighting your path to assertiveness!

Chapter 6. Fine-tuning Your Verbal Communication Skills

As an essential thread in the fabric of assertiveness, verbal communication plays a pivotal role in framing our discourse with the world around us. Our words carry weight, both in shaping our self-perception and in influencing how others perceive us. Understanding the magic of this often underestimated tool, and wielding it appropriately, can drastically metamorphize our interactions, making us catalysts in our own narrative rather than mere passive recipients of external circumstances.

6.1. The Essence of Verbal Communication

First, let's delve into the foundational understanding of verbal communication. At its very core, verbal communication is a two-way process of sharing thoughts, ideas, emotions, and information using spoken language. It stands as a glue binding us with individuals in our lives, highlighting our shared pursuits while skillfully managing our differences. Meticulous attention to the nuances of language can afford us the luxury of crafting a compelling personal and professional image.

However, fine-tuning verbal communication skills goes beyond adept language usage. It is as much about what you say as it is about how you say it. It invites a delicate infrastructure of clear articulation, concise expression, proper tone, grammatical accuracy, not skipping important contextual details, and fortitude in the face of disagreement.

6.2. Honing Articulation Skills

Articulation is the act of expressing your thoughts and ideas clearly and effectively. It is a practical mix of word choice, sentence construction, and clarity of thought. The first step towards improved articulation is expanding your vocabulary. This isn't about cultivating an arsenal of complex, fancy words to parade in dialogues, but about enriching your language to provide you with a diverse set of tools to express varied ideas and emotions. Reading widely, from contemporary literature to scientific texts, will help you drastically in this regard.

Next, it's vital to practice formulating complete, coherent sentences before speaking, particularly in formal contexts. Practicing this skill frequently, perhaps by explaining complex ideas or thoughts to a friend, can vastly improve your communication prowess. Finally, maintaining clarity of thought is crucial for articulate communication. This requires you to structure your thoughts coherently before translating them into words, making your speech crystal clear and easily digestible.

6.3. Emphasizing Tone and Inflection

The tone of voice wanders beyond the boundary of the words spoken, offering additional expressional depth to the spoken language. The importance of tone, inflection, and volume in effective communication channels often goes unnoticed, yet it aids in minimizing misunderstandings and building constructive conversation landscapes.

A soft-spoken tone implies gentleness and humility, whereas a firm tone can convey assertiveness and desire for control. Speaking hurriedly can imply nervousness, while a slower pace can exude confidence and calmness. Thus, manipulating the tone, pace, and volume of your speech depending upon the situation and audience can significantly control the perception of your message.

6.4. Mastering Language Accuracy

To command respect and credibility through communication, develop a keen sensitivity to language accuracy. Aim to uphold grammatical correctness and appropriate syntax, as sloppy grammar can mar your professional image. Simultaneously, steer clear of needless jargon or slang (unless contextually relevant) and make a conscious effort to employ the right semantics, particularly in cross-cultural conversations to prevent misunderstandings or misinterpretations.

6.5. Contextual Considerations

When communicating, we must unravel the importance of context. Conversations occur in a diverse array of scenarios, each one fostering a unique set of norms, expectations, and tone. A formal business discussion, an intimate chat with a friend, a heated debate, or a counselling session all call for a distinct approach to verbal communication.

Thus, fine-tuning your verbal communication skills also demands a keen awareness of your environment and audience. Wisely adjusting your communication approach without compromising your assertive stance can open the door to respect and progress.

6.6. Displaying Assertiveness in Disagreeable Situations

An important facet of verbal communication often overlooked is our ability to maintain assertiveness and respect in disagreeable situations or conflicts. Mastering this skill requires the precision of a tightrope walker, upholding your stance without trampling over others' perspectives. Practice speaking your mind without hostility, employing 'I' statements to express feelings, and employing thoughtful diplomacy. This wholesome communication approach humanizes disagreements, allowing your counterparts to 'hear' and respect your viewpoint without feeling attacked.

Fine-tuning verbal communication, then, is nothing short of choreographing a harmonious dance - you evolve with fluidity, cognizant of the space around you, respects your partners, and effectively express this engagement. The grace with which you blend your body language, tone, choice of words, and contextual sensitivity into your dialogue influences not just the response to your message but the very layers of your personal and professional relationships. This dance, when mastered, allows you to lead assertively, commanding respect, and nurturing holistic connections. Acknowledge your journey's ongoing nature, relishing the continued learning and growth process. After all, assertiveness is not just a skill to acquire, but a lifelong art to master!

Chapter 7. Non-Verbal Communication: The Silent Conductor of Respect

Non-verbal communication is a colossal and integral component of our daily interactions, wielding the power to elicit respect or, conversely, depreciate it. It's a universal language, transcending verbal dialects and cultural barriers, making it a silent yet influential conductor of respect. When words fall short or are contradicted by physical cues, it is non-verbal communication that speaks volumes, harmonizing the symphony of our interactions with profound resonance. Let's embark on a detailed exploration of this silent language that so eloquently manifests our inner sentiments to the observable world.

7.1. Unraveling Non-Verbal Communication

Non-verbal communication embraces a diverse spectrum, encompassing elements like body language, facial expressions, eye contact, gestures, physical distance, and even aspects like tone, pitch, and volume of voice, despite being technically 'unspoken'. Governing almost 93% of our communication, it's not just a supplement to our words, but a predominant and vital form of expressing our feelings, intentions, and assertions.

Understanding non-verbal cues provides us unparalleled insight into the unspoken thoughts and emotional states of others. Simultaneously, it allows us to control and refine our messages, ensuring optimum reception by our counterparts. The subtle cues we emit can become an arsenal of influence, fostering deep connections and respect in our interpersonal interactions.

7.2. The Semiotics of Body Language

Body language, termed Kinesics, is an elaborate study in itself. It deals with how body movements and posture interpret our feelings and thoughts. Unconscious but universal, we all partake in this expressive dance that augments our spoken dialogue, whether it's through a reassuring pat on the back, a confident handshake, or a dismissive shrug.

Indeed, our posture, gait, and movements narrate silent tales of our confidence levels, openness, engagement, and interest. A slumped posture, for instance, is often linked to low self-esteem or disinterest, while an erect, tall posture radiates assertiveness and courage. Understanding and refining these signs provide a direct route to galvanize respect from our peers.

7.3. The Power of Facial Expressions

Facial expressions constitute the most universal realm in non-verbal communication. Regardless of cultural diversity, certain emotions such as happiness, sadness, surprise, disgust, fear, and anger manifest universally and spontaneously on our faces. A warm smile broadcasts friendliness and openness; raised eyebrows express surprise or interest; while a furrowed brow can signal confusion or concern. Mastering the art of reading and controlling facial expressions renders us approachable and empathetic, fostering mutual respect in our dealings.

7.4. The Impact of Eye Contact

Eye contact, an essential element of non-verbal communication, serves as a potent tool for commanding respect. It can express acknowledgment, interest, attention, and even dominance. A steady but non-threatening gaze during conversations evokes trust and openness, making the recipient feel seen, heard, and valued. Conversely, avoiding eye contact can aggravate feelings of unease, mistrust, or disinterest. Harnessing the expressive potential of eye contact can significantly heighten our assertion and command respect in all interpersonal situations.

7.5. Navigating Personal Space and Proximity

Personal space can tell us a lot about a relationship without a single word being uttered. The distance we maintain from others, whether it's in professional or personal contexts, transmits signals about our comfort levels, relationship status, and intentions. Invading someone's space without implicit permission can elicit discomfort and disrespect, while maintaining appropriate distances illustrates respect for their personal boundaries.

7.6. Deciphering Gestures and Touch

Gestures, another facet of non-verbal communication, also bear profound impact. They add emphasis or illustrate our words, making our intentions clearer and our conversations more engaging. Moreover, the strategic use of touch, such as a gentle pat on the back or a firm, confident handshake, can exude warmth, encouragement, and confidence. However, it's crucial to ensure that all touch remains within comfortable and consensual boundaries to maintain respect.

7.7. The Resonance of Paralanguage

Paralanguage refers to the vocal components, excluding words, which are often overlooked but significantly impact how our verbal communication is received. Aspects like tone, speed, volume, and inflection can add a multitude of unsaid meanings to our words, enhancing or altering their reception. A soothing tone suggests kindness and empathy; a confident volume emanates assertiveness and strength; meanwhile, upward inflections can suggest uncertainty or lack of decisive confidence.

7.8. Bringing It All Together: Non-Verbal Assertiveness

All the elements of non-verbal communication coalesce to form compelling schemes of interaction, each piece fitting together like a jigsaw puzzle to create a complete picture. Understanding the interplay between these elements is paramount to mastering the art of non-verbal communication. Through conscious observation and practice, we can fine-tune our non-verbal cues to exude assertiveness, capture attention, and command respect.

To conclude, our non-verbal cues, those silent but resonant signals, interweave with our spoken words to project our personality to the world. Thus, consciously utilizing and interpreting such cues places enormous power at our disposal. This understanding paves the way for our ascendancy in our personal and professional spheres, commanding respect through the silent conductor - non-verbal communication. It's time we started speaking this universal language with intention and grace to manifest the respect and assertiveness we seek.

Remember, we say more when we aren't speaking at all. And in this silence, respect reverberates the loudest. So, hold the conductor's baton with confidence and let your non-verbal symphony play.

Chapter 8. Assertiveness in Conflict Resolution: Winning Without Fighting

Delving into the realm of conflict resolution, it becomes imperative to acknowledge the instrumental role assertiveness plays in mitigating conflict and establishing harmonious relationships. This chapter aims to further elucidate the benefits of assertiveness in conflict resolution, equipping you with practical strategies to win without fighting. Herein lies the art of assertive communication in managing disagreements - balancing respect for your own rights with an equal regard for others' rights, thereby fostering peace, cooperation, and mutual understanding without resorting to aggression.

8.1. Assertiveness: A Non-combative Approach

Assertiveness, in the context of conflict resolution, is a communicative approach that leads to fair and balanced outcomes. It involves asserting your ideas, perspectives, or needs in a way that respects others' viewpoints. Unlike aggressive communication, where you may trample others' rights, or passive communication, where you might ignore your stands, being assertive positions you in a middle ground. Assertiveness encourages an open dialogue about the issue at hand where everyone's perspectives are acknowledged and considered, fostering a solution that benefits all parties.

8.2. The Psychology of Assertive Conflict Resolution

The assertive approach to conflict resolution is deeply rooted in psychology. This methodology relies on empathy – understanding and acknowledging others' emotional states and perspectives. By expressing yourself assertively, you validate both your feelings and the feelings of the person you are in conflict with. You maintain a balance between emotional intelligence and logical reasoning, thus including compassion in your communication.

8.3. The Techniques of Assertive Conflict Resolution

Realigning your habits to include assertive behavior during conflicts can significantly enhance your interactions. To this end, the art of assertive conflict resolution revolves around a few proven techniques.

1. *Active Listening:* Active listening is an essential skill in effective commotion management. It involves hearing out the other person's perspective without preparing your response or verdict, being fully engaged in what they're expressing. It enables you to understand the core of the problem and empathize with their viewpoint.
2. *Clear Communication:* Clarity is key when asserting your views. Avoid vague jargon, assumptions, and accusations. Instead, express your thoughts and feelings directly, focusing on the issue and avoiding personal attacks or blame games.
3. *I-statements:* Using I-statements instead of You-statements can make your claims seem less accusative. For instance, instead of saying, "You never understand what I mean!", you could say, "I feel misunderstood when I express my thoughts."

4. *Say No Wisely:* Knowing when and how to say no assertively helps maintain your boundaries without offending others.
5. *Non-verbal Assertiveness:* Your body language can either reinforce or undermine your verbal assertiveness. Maintain direct eye contact, adopt an open body posture, and modulate your voice accordingly to convey assertiveness non-verbally.

8.4. Conflict Resolution Styles: Comparison with Assertiveness

Understanding the difference between various conflict resolution styles, namely, avoidance, accommodation, competition, compromise, and collaboration, can lead to informed choices on when to employ assertiveness as an effective tool. While assertiveness forms the core of compromise and collaboration, understanding when to use these over other styles can drastically improve your conflict resolution.

8.5. Practical Tips on Incorporating Assertiveness in Conflict Management

Building assertiveness as a conflict resolution skill is a journey that involves constant practice and conscious adjustments. Among practical steps you can undertake include practicing alone before confrontation, constantly seeking constructive feedback, and never being too harsh on yourself when initial attempts do not yield perfect results.

In conclusion, assertive conflict resolution is not about winning or losing, but rather about reaching a mutual understanding and resolution that respects all parties involved. As we continue to explore the contours of assertiveness, let's delve into the fascinating realm of professional respect in the following chapter.

Chapter 9. Cultivating Respect in Professional Spaces

Our journey to cultivate respect in professional spaces not only transforms how we perceive ourselves, but also changes how others perceive us. By grounding our interaction in assertiveness, we pave the way for the reciprocal exchange of respect and understanding. In this chapter, we'll meticulously explore the numerous facets of cultivating respect within professional environments.

9.1. Setting Expectations and Boundaries

To foster a culture of respect at your workplace, setting clear expectations and firm boundaries serves as the baseline. Without these, we leave the door ajar for misunderstanding, disputes and a potential dent in the professional rapport. Let's understand navigating these complexities from a deep-grounded, psychological perspective. The strength here doesn't lie in avoiding difficulties, rather in understanding their essence and asserting our position confidently yet empathetically.

9.2. Assertive Communication: The Professional Power Tool

Building respectful relationships in professional settings, is no less than crafting a piece of art. And a painting is only as good as the strokes you draw. Assertive communication is one such brush to color the canvas of your workplace with respect. It is not merely about speaking up or making others understand your point. It's about a balanced blend of clearly stating your thoughts while showing empathy for others' perspectives—the ethos of assertive communication.

9.3. The Power of Active Listening

Active listening is an underestimated tool in the toolbox of professional respect. It isn't about just merely hearing, it's about attentively understanding and making your peers feel valued. It's a bridge connecting the realm of empathy and assertiveness. While the importance of speaking up should not be understated, the power to listen and show understanding to our colleagues is the axis around which the globe of respect revolves.

9.4. Displaying Empathy in Conflict Resolution

In professional spaces, conflict is as inevitable as the rising sun. However, what makes us stand out as admirable is our capacity to handle conflict with empathy. Empathy fuels our ability to put ourselves in others' shoes, understand their predicaments and finding plausible solutions, establishing us as respectful and valued team members.

9.5. Building a Leadership Persona

A leader is not merely a position—it's an attitude underscored by assertion and respect. Leadership is not about dominating; rather, it's about harnessing, guiding, and growing the team dynamics positively. Building a leadership persona contrary to popular opinion isn't about bossism; it is about standing tall on the pillars of trust, assertiveness and respect.

9.6. Assertiveness and Team Dynamics

Teams are the lifeblood of professional spaces. However, fostering a harmonious team requires efforts. This is where the art of assertiveness plays an integral role. Assertiveness ensures that all team members can voice their thoughts and ideas without fear of rebuff, creating a fertile breeding ground for innovation, collaboration and most importantly—respect.

9.7. Assertive Email Communication

In an increasingly digital world, your written communication is as important as spoken. Be it a humble email or an official letter, your words can leave imprints. Assertiveness embedded in your writing can transform your image from being a passive professional to a proactive, respectful leader.

By exploring these essentials of cultivating respect in professional spaces, you'd be empowered to navigate a professional environment differently. This chapter is not merely about tips and tricks, but about providing you the key to unlock a wholistic professional transformation—a metamorphosis from being perceived as a part of the crowd to becoming a beacon commanding respect. From understanding the psychology behind respect to harnessing the power of assertive communication, it all comes down to the courage to cultivate an aura of respect in the professional spaces. As we traverse these topics, remember, this is more about growth and less about perfection—each step forward in this journey will help you unveil the power of assertiveness, commanding respect, and transforming your professional life.

Chapter 10. Elevating Personal Relationships With Assertiveness

Elevating personal relationships through the application of assertiveness can feel like navigating a labyrinth, filled with unique surprises at every corner. But fear not! As your experienced guide, we aim to turn this UX into a strategic game-plan, synergistically integrating scientifically robust theories with actionable practices to supercharge your relationship dynamics. Hang tight as we delve deep into this magnetic combination of psychology, communication skills, and emotional intelligence, propelling you towards a vibrant destiny of enriched personal connections.

10.1. Understanding Assertiveness in Personal Relationships

Assertiveness may often be pigeonholed into a profession-oriented skill set. However, this misconception could not be farther from truth! Its application seeps into every human interaction, including day-to-day personal relationships. Whether it's your interactions with a lifelong partner, childhood friends, or beloved family members, assertiveness stands as a cornerstone. It facilitates clear, effective, and respectful communication, fostering an environment marked by mutual understanding and shared empathy - key attributes of flourishing relationships. Remember, assertiveness is not about being aggressive or confrontation-driven; in essence, it revolves around your rights in a respectful and intentional manner, while simultaneously considering and respecting the rights of others.

10.2. The Power of "I" Statements in Assertiveness

One simple yet profound way to practice assertiveness in relationships is through "I" statements. This is a form of communication that focuses on the feelings or beliefs of the speaker rather than thoughts and characteristics that the speaker attributes to the listener. By shifting the emphasis in conversations from the behavior of the other person to your feelings or perspective, "I" statements can significantly reduce the potential for conflict. Negative feelings might be defused, mutual understanding could emerge, and room for compassionate response may be created.

Here's a simple syntax for "I" statements: "I feel [emotion] when [specific behavior] because [reason]. I need [what you want/need]." It is worth practicing this structure until it feels natural in your conversations. It's an inicial tool to draw from when emotions run high.

10.3. Implementing Assertiveness in Relationship Conflicts

The stage of relationship conflicts often puts assertiveness to the test. In such a time, resorting to our default, less-than-ideal communication styles - be it aggression, submission or avoidance - might be tempting. However, the assertive approach serves better; it involves an equal regard for your rights and feelings, and those of your partner.

In conflict situations, it is important to keep open lines of communication, express your thoughts, feelings, and needs openly and honestly, listen empathically to your partner's perspective, and negotiate a solution that respects both parties' rights and needs. Using "I" statements, as mentioned above, could also play an indispensable role here.

10.4. The Impact of Non-Verbal Assertiveness in Personal Relationships

Just as crucial as the words you speak is your non-verbal communication when asserting your thoughts and feelings. Your body language, facial expressions, eye contact, and tone of voice are integral elements in the communication process, often revealing more than words might express.

In your quest for assertiveness, strive to match your body language with your words. Maintain friendly yet confident eye contact, use a calm and clear tone of voice, adopt open body language, respect personal space and use touch appropriately. It is only when verbal and non-verbal communication work in harmony that your message will be effective and decisive, demonstrating your assertive stance.

10.5. Sustaining Assertive Communication in Personal Relationships

While knowing the principles and tools of assertive communication is an essential first step, the real challenge lies in making it a way of life in your personal relationships. It requires practice, patience, and persistence. Some people might be taken aback by your newfound assertiveness, while others may appreciate the clarity it brings. In either case, you must stick to it, adapting as necessary, but maintaining your assertive essence.

Remember, assertiveness in personal relationships is not a one-size-fits-all scheme. It's a dynamic process, adapting to the specifics of each relationship on your personal journey. Navigating this transformation can undeniably be a stimulating, albeit challenging task. But keep in mind, through the winding routes and the steep slopes, an elevated destination awaits - a life replete with enriched personal relationships that let you be authentically you, respectfully listened to, validated, and valued for the unique individual that you are.

And thus, we conclude this exhaustive treatise on elevating personal relationships with assertiveness - a kernel of knowledge and wisdom born from the marriage of research and real-life explorations. Knit these pieces together, adopt them in your life, and experience the remarkable transformations it brings in your personal relationships!

Chapter 11. Sustaining Your Assertive Journey: Maintaining Momentum and Progress

We begin our final chapter by indulging in reflection, a critical component that has undoubtedly played a part in your journey to assertiveness. The road to sustaining any transformation, including developing assertiveness, is a winding one paved with diligence, evaluation, refreshment of strategies, and persistence. Throughout this chapter, we will traverse the landscapes of reflective practice, maintenance strategies, and progress assessment to ensure the longevity of your assertive journey.

11.1. Reflective Practice: Evaluating Your Experiences

Reflective practice is an active and deliberate process of retrospection aimed at evaluating experiences and identifying areas for potential growth. The art of reflection is intrinsically linked to progress, as one cannot proceed on a development path without considering which aspects require further honing or refining. A reflection-focused mindset encourages conscious learning about oneself and the environment, fostering a feedback loop that directly contributes to enhancing assertiveness and thus, commanding respect.

Reflective practice generally involves three primary phases: introspection, investigation, and implementation.

The first phase, *introspection*, is all about creating the 'you' database -

a collection of your thoughts, behaviors, beliefs, reactions, and achievements. It calls for sincerity and open-mindedness to evaluate your actions objectively and identify the patterns impacting your growth trajectory. The second phase, *investigation*, takes the 'you' database and scrutinizes each observation under a developmental lens, attempting to draw connections, devise strategies, or formulate alternative approaches. The third phase, *implementation*, gears you up for action. Here, the insights gathered from the first two steps are converted into real-world strategies, refined over time to optimize their effectiveness in maintaining momentum and progressing assertiveness capabilities.

As you scoop out the lessons of your past, you strengthen the cornerstone of your growth, and pave the way for a more evolved self.

11.2. Maintenance Strategies: Keeping the Momentum Alive

Assertiveness, no matter how well-learned or mastered, may dim under the weight of complacency, making maintenance strategies indispensable to its longevity. These strategies consist, among other elements, of:

1. Regularly **practicing assertiveness skills** in diverse situations to apply learned concepts, challenge your understanding, and accustom your mind to new reaction patterns.
2. **Seeking constructive feedback** from peers, colleagues, or mentors who can provide a different perspective, point out areas for improvement, and reaffirm your growth.
3. Staying updated with current **research on assertiveness and communication strategies**, keeping your knowledge fresh and ideas up-to-date.
4. **Physical exercises and mindfulness activities** such as yoga,

meditation, or even simple stretching, which can aid in stress management, enhance concentration, and improve overall well-being, indirectly boosting your assertiveness.

However, maintenance should not feel like drudgery. Add variety to these activities to make them enjoyable and integrate them seamlessly into your existing lifestyle. Remember, you're building sustainability, grounding your newly attained assertiveness into a robust, lifelong skill.

11.3. Tracking Your Progress: Navigating the Assertiveness Map

As you journey through the assertiveness landscape, the metaphorical map that guides you is Progress. Tracking progress is not about measuring success or failure; instead, it serves as a compass, revealing where you are and indicating the route towards your next milestone.

Tracking progress may seem arduous, but it need not be. It can be as simple as maintaining an assertiveness journal where entries record your daily encounters, the application of assertiveness skills, your reactions, others' responses, and any lessons learned. Simple tools such as SWOT analyses (Strengths, Weaknesses, Opportunities, Threats) or even digital apps offering reflective prompts could also help to record and interpret your journey.

When tracking progress, it's important to celebrate wins, however small, and be kind to yourself during losses or stagnation. After all, growth often involves a few stumbles and setbacks. Resilience and perseverance, not perfection, should be your companions on this exciting journey.

A parting thought for this transformative voyage - staying assertive and commanding respect are not solitary endeavors but an enthralling dance between finding your voice and resonating with others. A dance that requires grace, not brute force; empathy, not greed; integrity, not deception; and most importantly, the audacity to stumble, rise, and keep moving forward. As we conclude this chapter and, indeed, this comprehensive guide, remember that every interaction is a chance to learn, grow, and dance the transformative dance of assertiveness.

www.ingramcontent.com/pod-product-compliance
Lightning Source LLC
Chambersburg PA
CBHW070951220526
45471CB00007B/2979